Profiles of the Presidents

HERBERT
HOOVER

★ ★ ★

LOCUST VALLEY LIBRARY

Profiles of the Presidents

HERBERT HOOVER

by Michael Teitelbaum

Content Advisers: Dr. Timothy Walch, Director, and Mary Evans, Education Specialist, Hoover Presidential Library, West Branch, Iowa

Reading Adviser: Dr. Linda D. Labbo, Department of Reading Education, College of Education, The University of Georgia

COMPASS POINT BOOKS ✦ MINNEAPOLIS, MINNESOTA

Compass Point Books
3722 West 50th Street, #115
Minneapolis, MN 55410

Visit Compass Point Books on the Internet at *www.compasspointbooks.com*
or e-mail your request to *custserv@compasspointbooks.com*

Photographs ©: Hulton/Archive by Getty Images, cover, 3, 20, 21, 24 (all), 27, 28, 29, 31, 32
(bottom), 33, 34, 36, 40, 43, 55 (right), 57 (left); Herbert Hoover Presidential Library and Museum,
6, 8 (all), 9, 10, 11, 12, 13, 15, 16, 17, 23 (all), 54 (left), 55 (top left), 56 (top & bottom left);
Franklin D. Roosevelt Library, 7, 42, 46, 58 (bottom right); Bettmann/Corbis, 14, 25, 38, 48, 50, 55
(bottom left), 58(left); Corbis, 18, 19, 35, 49, 56 (middle left), 59 (left); Library of Congress, 26;
Stock Montage, 32 (top), 37, 41, 45, 58 (top right); The Denver Public Library, Western History
Collection, 39, 54 (right); E.O. Hoppe/Corbis, 57 (right); Galen Rowell/Corbis, 59 (right).

Editors: E. Russell Primm, Emily J. Dolbear, Melissa McDaniel, and Catherine Neitge
Photo Researcher: Svetlana Zhurkina
Photo Selector: Linda S. Koutris
Designer: The Design Lab
Cartographer: XNR Productions, Inc.

Library of Congress Cataloging-in-Publication Data

Teitelbaum, Michael.
  Herbert Hoover / by Michael Teitelbaum.
     v. cm.— (Profiles of the presidents)
 Includes bibliographical references and index.
 Contents: The great humanitarian and the Great Depression—Growing up—The Stanford years—
First jobs —Traveling the world—World War I and the Committee for the Relief of Belgium—The
U.S. enters the War, Hoover Feeds the World—A Cabinet Post—President Hoover—After the White
House— Glossary—Herbert Hoover's life at a glance—Herbert Hoover's life and times—World
events—Understanding Herbert Hoover and His Presidency.
  ISBN 0-7565-0277-2
  1. Hoover, Herbert, 1874–1964—Juvenile literature. 2. Presidents—United States—Biography—
Juvenile literature. [1. Hoover, Herbert, 1874–1964. 2. Presidents.] I. Title. II. Series.
  E802 .T37 2003
  973.91'6'092—dc21   2002003017

© 2003 by Compass Point Books

All rights reserved. No part of this book may be reproduced without written permission from the
publisher. The publisher takes no responsibility for the use of any of the materials or methods
described in this book, nor for the products thereof.

Printed in the United States of America.

Table of Contents

★ ★ ★

The Great Man and the Great Depression

★ ★ ★

Before he became president, Herbert Hoover was one of the most admired men in the United States. In those days he was known as the Great **Humanitarian,** because he had done so much to help others.

Early in World War I (1914–1918), Hoover was in charge of the Commission for Relief in Belgium (CRB). The CRB fed millions of hungry people in Europe. These

Hoover spent much of his life trying to help hungry children all over the world.

people would have starved without Hoover's help. After the war ended, Hoover headed the American Relief Administration, which fed 300 million people across Europe and the Middle East.

Hoover's presidency, however, is remembered for the terrible time in American history called the Great Depression. During those years—the early 1930s—the nation's economy crumbled. People lost their jobs and their homes. Many Americans went hungry. Because of the Great Depression, this very popular man went down in history as one of the least-liked presidents.

▾ *The Great Depression left many Americans without jobs or homes.*

Growing Up

★ ★ ★

Herbert Clark Hoover was born on August 10, 1874, in the small town of West Branch, Iowa. His father, Jesse Hoover, was the town blacksmith. His mother, Hulda Minthorn Hoover, worked as a teacher and a seamstress. Herbert's parents and friends usually called him Bert, for short. Herbert had an older brother, Theodore, known as Tad. Herbert's younger sister, Mary, was called May.

Bert, Tad, and May enjoyed hiking, swimming, and searching for fossils in the gravel near their home. Bert also liked fishing in summer and sledding on a homemade sled in winter.

Herbert's mother, ▶
Hulda

Herbert's father, ▶
Jesse

8

The Hoover family, like most people in West Branch, were **Quakers.** The Quakers are a Christian group who believe in peace, hard work, education, charity, and good planning. All these qualities would help Bert develop into a man who would one day become a major world leader. Herbert's mother was a recorded minister who often spoke at Quaker meetings.

▲ *The Hoover children: Theodore, left, Herbert, and Mary.*

Tragedy struck Bert at an early age. In 1880, when Bert was six, his father died. Jesse Hoover was only thirty-four years old. Just more than three years later, at the age of thirty-five, Herbert's mother died. After their mother's death, May went to live with Grandmother Minthorn, and Tad went to live with his uncle John Minthorn. Herbert lived with his uncle Allan Hoover for almost two years. Then he was sent west to live with another uncle—Dr. Henry John Minthorn—in Newberg, Oregon.

Herbert eventually ▸
came to live with
his Uncle Henry in
this house in
Newberg, Oregon.

Besides going to school, eleven-year-old Bert worked very hard at his uncle's home. He fed the horses, milked the cows, split logs for the stove, and helped clear a forest of fir trees. Although his life was not as carefree as it had been when his parents were alive, Bert didn't mind all the hard work. He grew strong from doing the many chores, and he was a good student.

When Bert was fourteen, his uncle opened a real estate office in Salem, Oregon. Bert went to work there. He quickly learned typing, bookkeeping, and other skills. Soon, the bright young man had learned every part of his uncle's business. While still working in his uncle's office during the day, Bert began attending business college at night. Soon, he would go off to college full time.

Bert's brother, Tad, had gone to a Quaker college, and his uncle wanted Bert to do the same thing. Bert had become more interested in **geology** and **engineering,** however. When a visiting professor told Bert about a brand-new university called Stanford, he decided to go there instead. Students did not have to pay for classes at Stanford, and the school offered many engineering and geology courses. Bert's uncle finally agreed. In the summer of 1891, Bert left Oregon for Palo Alto, California, to attend Stanford.

Bert (as he preferred to be called) Hoover began going to Stanford the year that university opened. He chose to study geology. Later, he decided he wanted to become a

▾ *Hoover, second from left, and Dr. Branner's Stanford geology class*

mining engineer. His geology teacher, Dr. John Caspar Branner, soon offered him a part-time job. So Hoover put his typing skills to work in the Geology Department's office. The money he made helped pay for his room and board. Hoover also earned money delivering newspapers and doing laundry. In the summers, he mapped rock formations in California and Arkansas.

Hoover had worked long hours from the time he was eleven. As a result, he had never spent much time

Hoover ▶ with fellow Stanford students in 1893

Arthur Diggles   R E McDonnell
Herbert Hoover   James White
SURVEYING SQUAD - STANFORD UNIVERSITY IN 1893

making friends or socializing. He was shy, but blunt. It took some time for people to warm up to him.

In his senior year, Hoover met a student named Lou Henry, the only woman in the Geology Department. She was warm, athletic, and adventurous. She also shared Hoover's love of fishing and the outdoors. By the time Hoover left Stanford, they had decided to get married. But they would wait until he could afford to support a family.

Hoover graduated from Stanford in May 1895. He had a degree in geology and $40 in his pocket. Because he had worked all through college, Hoover had no debts when he graduated. He was ready to begin his life in the world of business.

▾ *Lou Henry while on a geology field trip*

Traveling the World

★   ★   ★

Hoover during his ▼
days as an
engineer in the
mining business

Herbert Hoover learned the mining business from the ground up. His first mining job involved pushing a car full of ore on the lowest levels of the Reward Gold Mine in California. He worked a ten-hour shift, deep underground, for $1.50 to $2 per day.

When work at this mine slowed down, Hoover had to look for other work. He found a job as a typist with Louis Janin, an expert on mining in the West. Hoover impressed Janin greatly. He moved up quickly in the company. Each new job carried greater responsibility than the last.

In the fall of 1896, Janin told Hoover about a job with Bewick, Moreing and Company, a British mining firm. The firm was looking for American mining engineers. They wanted people skilled in gold mining to work in Western Australia.

Hoover was just twenty-three years old. He had been working as an engineer for less than two years. He was worried that he was too young and did not have enough experience. But Janin encouraged him to interview for the job. In March 1897, Hoover sailed to London to meet his new employers. By May he had arrived in Western Australia. From there he traveled inland by train to the hot and dusty Coolgardie mining

◀ *A mining team in Coolgardie, Australia*

settlement. Hoover later said, "It is a land of red dust, black flies, and white heat."

At first Hoover worked on the technical side of mining. He studied the rocks and the landscape. But he soon rose into the management ranks of the company and became one of its most valued employees.

Charles Moreing, one of the company's owners, thought very highly of Hoover. Moreing offered Hoover the chance to go to China to help run the firm's mining operations there. A higher salary would come with the new job.

Herbert and Lou ▾ Henry Hoover on their wedding day in 1899

Hoover accepted the offer. Now that he was making more money, he felt it was finally time to marry Lou Henry. Hoover returned to the United States just long enough for their wedding in Lou's hometown of Monterey, California.

Right after the wedding, Herbert

and Lou boarded a train that took them to a boat. That boat carried them off to their new life together in China.

During his time in Australia, Hoover had learned a great deal about mining technology and management. He would put these skills to good use in China. He would also come face to face with a political **rebellion.**

A group of Chinese people known as Boxers wanted to destroy everything foreign in China. This included railroads, houses, and people. In June 1900, the Boxer rebellion erupted. For four weeks, the Hoovers were trapped in the old city of Tianjin.

◄ *Lou Henry Hoover and her husband were trapped in Tianjin during the Boxer rebellion.*

During that time, Hoover directed the building of walls to help defend the city from the Boxers. He also saw that food and water were given to the 600 Chinese who were trapped in the old city with the foreigners. His leadership skills grew with each passing day.

In August 1900, the Hoovers left China but they later returned. Hoover did very well with Bewick, Moreing and Company and, by 1902, the company made him a junior partner. This new job meant a lot of travel for Herbert and Lou. His career was in full swing now, and his responsibilities grew. Soon, his family would grow, too.

Hoover was a ▾ successful businessman, and this 1901 poster describes him as the highest salaried man of his age in the world.

THE HIGHEST
SALARIED MAN
OF HIS AGE IN
THE WORLD

From 1902 to 1907, the Hoovers traveled a great deal by ship and train, circling the globe five times. Herbert Hoover kept an eye on the company's operations around the world. He reviewed business deals and worked as a geologist and engineer. His reputation was growing. Soon he earned the nickname the "Great Engineer."

In 1903, the Hoovers were in London, England. It was there that their first child, Herbert Junior, was born. Within weeks, the newborn joined his parents as they set out on another long journey. In 1907, the couple's second child, Allan, was born in London. He, too, began his life traveling with the family.

Over time, Hoover became unhappy working with Bewick, Moreing and Company. He often disagreed with his business partner, Charles Moreing, about important decisions. In 1908, he left to start his own engineering company. His reputation as the Great Engineer, and his skill in managing money and people helped the new business grow quickly.

▼ *Herbert Hoover with little Herbert Junior*

Herbert Hoover had started out as a poor orphan. Through his hard work and determination, he began his own success-ful business. He also had a family he adored. But his greatest chal-lenges lay ahead.

Feeding the World

★   ★   ★

The Hoovers were living in London in 1914. That August, war broke out in Europe. As part of its attack on France, the German army marched through Belgium. Germany took control of the tiny nation. The Germans also took control of its food supply. Soon nearly everyone in the country was starving.

The German Army parades through Brussels, Belgium, during World War I.

Britain declared war on Germany. The British sent their powerful navy to **blockade** the European coast. This stopped Germany from sending out any warships. It also

stopped food and supplies from getting into areas controlled by Germany, such as Belgium. The British were

▲ *A German warship*

afraid that any food sent in to feed the hungry Belgians
would end up feeding German soldiers.

The starving people of Belgium needed help. A
group of American **diplomats** and Belgian business leaders began looking for someone to lead a relief effort.
They needed someone from a strong **neutral** country—
one that was not involved in the war. They needed
someone who had experience dealing with foreign governments and difficult situations. That person had to be

able to put together a large organization and find a lot of food and money—in a hurry.

They asked Herbert Hoover to take on this giant task. Hoover agreed. He would have complete control over the Commission for Relief in Belgium (CRB). It would be his biggest challenge to date. Hoover refused to accept any money for his work. "I could not appeal to others to **sacrifice** without sacrifice myself," he said.

The job was huge. Hoover had to find enough food to feed 10 million people every day. He had to find trucks, ships, and trains to carry the food. He had to find some way to **distribute** the food. And, of course, he had to find the money to pay for it all.

Hoover brought many strengths to the job. He used his technical knowledge as an engineer. He used his background in finding simple solutions to difficult problems. He also relied on the great **moral** strength he had developed during his Quaker upbringing.

Hoover went to Germany to talk to German officials. He persuaded the German government to agree to allow the food into Belgium. Then he raised money from governments and private citizens around the world. He also convinced Germany and the nations it was fighting that

the CRB was neutral. It was not concerned with taking sides in the war. It was simply concerned with feeding hungry people.

Even after the CRB started sending food, Belgian children were still not getting good nutrition. So the CRB made a special cookie containing all the vitamins children need each day. Hoover's greatest joy in the relief effort was seeing Belgian children grow healthy again. It was the beginning of his lifelong commitment to the well-being of children around the world.

▲ A supply ship carried food and supplies as a part of the Commission for Relief in Belgium. The huge banner helped guarantee safe passage.

▲ A Belgian classroom was transformed into a feeding center for children.

Walter H. ▶
Page spoke
highly of
Hoover.

President ▶
Woodrow
Wilson

Hoover's CRB fed 10 million people in Belgium and northern France for four years. It raised more than $1 billion to support the effort. Walter Hines Page, the U.S. **ambassador** to Britain, told President Woodrow Wilson that Hoover was a "simple, modest, energetic little man who began his career in California and will end it in Heaven, and he doesn't want anyone's thanks."

Many groups wanted to honor Hoover for his work with the CRB. Hoover refused to accept the honors. He believed the success of the CRB was enough of a reward.

World War I had been raging in Europe for almost three years before the United States got involved. On April 6, 1917, German submarines attacked U.S. ships, and the United States declared war on Germany.

▲ *A German submarine attacking an American ship*

In May, President Wilson asked Hoover to return to the United States to head the U.S. Food Administration. Wilson believed that Hoover's amazing success with the CRB made him the perfect person for the job. Hoover accepted the position. Once again, he would have complete control over the agency and, once again, he would accept no salary.

Hoover knew there was much work to be done. The United States had to feed its own troops, of course. The

U.S. FOOD
ADMINISTRATION

EAT MORE
CORN, OATS AND RYE
PRODUCTS —   FISH
AND POULTRY —   FRUITS,
VEGETABLES AND POTATOES
BAKED, BOILED AND
BROILED FOODS

EAT LESS
WHEAT, MEAT, SUGAR AND FATS
TO SAVE FOR THE ARMY
AND OUR ALLIES

A poster from ▲
the U.S Food
Administration
listing items that
Americans needed
to conserve

nation also needed to provide food for the armies of its **allies.** In World War I, U.S. allies included France and Britain. The people of the United States and its allies also had to be fed during those difficult times.

Hoover had to make sure everyone had enough to eat. He called his efforts "conservation." Americans soon began calling it "Hooverizing." Hoover started programs such as "Wheatless Wednesdays" and "Meatless Mondays." No one *had* to follow these programs, however. Hoover was against making laws that would force people to cut down on food.

His faith in the American people paid off. People did as he asked and conserved food. The slogan "Food Will Win the War" was heard around the country.

Hoover's agency controlled what kinds of crops farmers produced, how much they were paid, and where the food went. Soldiers were fed, and an extra supply of food was stored to prevent widespread hunger in Europe when the fighting stopped.

When the war ended in November 1918, President Wilson sent Hoover

▼ *A poster encouraging Americans to conserve food as part of the war effort*

FEED a FIGHTER
Eat only what you need—
Waste nothing—
That he and his family
may have enough

to Europe to find out how much food was needed there. Hoover discovered that Europe was in very bad shape, and many people were hungry.

The agency he headed was renamed the American Relief Administration (ARA). It soon became the main source of food for 300 million people in twenty-one countries in Europe and the Middle East. The ARA's work officially ended in 1923. Then Hoover set up the ARA European Children's Fund to make sure that children across Europe continued to be fed.

Hoover felt it was important to feed anyone who was hungry, including the defeated Germans. Some European nations disagreed. They formed a blockade to prevent food

Bread was ▶ distributed to starving Europeans.

from reaching Germany. "Young man, I don't understand why you Americans want to feed these Germans," a British admiral said to Hoover. "Old man," Hoover replied bluntly, "I don't understand why you British want to starve women and children after they are licked."

By 1921, Russia was in the midst of a severe food shortage. Some Americans complained about feeding the Russians, whose political system was so different from that of the United States. Hoover had an answer: "Twenty million people are starving. Whatever their politics, they should be fed." Driven by his morality, Hoover put political differences aside. Once again, his only concern was feeding the hungry.

◀ *American relief workers in Russia*

Working in Washington

★ ★ ★

Hoover soon returned to his mining business. He and Lou also built their dream house—in California, near Stanford. Public service soon came calling again, however.

People in both the Democratic and Republican Parties wanted Hoover to run for president. Hoover declared that he was a Republican. Some Republican leaders, though, did not want Hoover to run. They felt that he was too much of a political outsider.

Republican Warren G. Harding was elected president in 1920. This was the first presidential election after World War I ended. Harding promised to return American life to "normal" as quickly as possible. The new president offered Herbert Hoover the position of secretary of commerce, and Hoover accepted.

Hoover immediately began expanding the Commerce Department, which deals with U.S. trade

and other business issues. In earlier years, this department was a mostly inactive part of the government.
Hoover would turn it into a department that helped
many Americans.

One of Hoover's great accomplishments was getting
industries to **standardize** their products. He saw that
U.S. companies were making too many sizes and types
of the same item. Hoover thought this was wasteful. If
all companies made their products the same size they
would be cheaper to make—and to buy. It would also
make life easier for consumers. Among the many items

▼ *President Warren
G. Harding*

Hoover helped stan-
dardize were nuts and
bolts, paper, automo-
bile tires, plumbing
pipes, window frames,
and lightbulbs.

Under Hoover,
the Commerce
Department encour-
aged people to use
new technology to
improve American

life. Lighthouses began using radio beacons to signal ships. Hoover pushed the Post Office to use airplanes to carry mail across the country. He also introduced safety standards for elevators and automobile brakes. His department ordered the use of runway lights at airports to make night flying safer.

Hoover also organized a group of seven states to work together to develop a plan to share

Hoover works an amateur radio during his term as secretary of commerce, which began in 1921.

Hoover encouraged the post office to use airplanes to deliver mail.

the water of the Colorado River. As a result, a huge dam was built on the river at the Arizona–Nevada border. The dam controlled flooding, produced electricity, and brought water to dry farmlands. Years later, it would become known as Hoover Dam.

◄ *Hoover Dam*

During the 1920s, Hoover continued to help children. He raised money to promote health education for children. He wrote the Child's Bill of Rights and argued for the use of vaccines to protect children against deadly diseases such as smallpox and diphtheria. He also helped start programs to feed American children who were not getting enough to eat.

President Calvin ▼
Coolidge, left, Secretary of the Treasury Andrew W. Mellon, and Secretary of Commerce Herbert Hoover

In 1923, President Harding died. His vice president, Calvin Coolidge, became president. The following year, Coolidge won his first elected term as president. He asked Hoover to stay on as secretary of commerce, and Hoover agreed.

President Coolidge announced in 1928 that he would not run for another term. Right away, Herbert Hoover received a flood of letters and telegrams asking him to run for president. This time, the Republican Party was happy to have him run.

For President — HERBERT HOOVER

For Vice President — CHARLES CURTIS

◄ *Presidential candidate Herbert Hoover and running mate Charles Curtis*

President Hoover

★　★　★

In the 1928 presidential election, Hoover easily beat Democrat Alfred E. Smith, the governor of New York. On March 4, 1929, Hoover took office as the thirty-first president of the United States.

"We want to see a nation built of home-owners and farm own-ers," Hoover said in his **inaugural address,** the first such speech ever broadcast nationally.

Democrat Alfred ▶
E. Smith

"We want to see them in steady jobs. We want them all secure. I have no fears for the future of our country. It is bright with hope."

A typical day at the White House for President Hoover began at 7:30 A.M. with some exercise. After breakfast, he would work for half an hour in his office on letters, papers, or writing speeches. He then had

▲ Hoover is sworn in as president.

appointments every fifteen minutes until lunchtime. Hoover always had guests for lunch to discuss business. He spent his afternoons writing and attending more meetings. He left his office at six and had dinner with guests.

When Hoover became president, he had high hopes and big plans. He wanted to buy land for national parks. He hoped to improve water transportation and conditions

Herbert and Lou ▼ Henry Hoover greet U.S. veterans on June 10, 1931.

in prisons. He also planned to provide better health care and education for Native Americans.

On October 29, 1929, just a few months after he took office, many of his dreams died. The dreams of millions of other Americans died, too. On that day, the stock market crashed. The United States began its plunge into the worst economic crisis in its history—the Great Depression.

▲ *Hoover wanted to create better health care and education for Native Americans.*

People were both shocked and frightened when the stock market crashed in 1929.

The stock market had been soaring for much of the 1920s. Many people thought this growth would go on forever. Even people who couldn't afford to invest in the stock market were borrowing money to buy stock. When they got nervous that the stock market would stop rising, they sold their stocks. More than 16 million shares of stock were sold on October 29—a day that came to be known as Black Tuesday.

Many people who paid a lot for their stocks had to sell them for very low prices. Those who had borrowed money to buy stocks could not afford to pay it back. All of a sudden, the future looked very dark.

People were worried about keeping their jobs and having enough money. They stopped buying new cars, houses, and others products. This meant that factories did not need to produce as much, so the companies needed fewer workers. Offices, factories, and stores began laying off workers. Many people had no money and no job.

◀ Like many other businesses, this Iowa bank closed as a result of the stock market crash.

Americans waited ▲
in bread lines
to get a meal.

President Hoover was blamed for the country's problems. People lost confidence in the man who had done so much for the United States and the world. They began to ask for direct aid from the government. This was against Hoover's belief in helping people help themselves.

In 1930, a terrible drought hit the Midwest, adding to the nation's problems. Without rain, crops died in the fields, and many farmers lost their land. The hard times kept getting harder.

By 1931, Hoover had agreed to help the farmers. He also agreed to ship food to poor areas around the country. Out-of-work people waited in long lines for bread and other basic needs.

Hoover also tried to help in other ways. To give people jobs, the federal government began projects such as building roads. Hoover's critics called this wasteful. It seemed that no matter what he did to try to pull the nation out of the Great Depression, someone said it was wrong, or that it was not enough.

▼ *A political cartoon criticized Hoover's policies.*

1928: Elected 31st president of the United States.

1874: Born in West Branch, Iowa

1891–1895: Attends Stanford University as part of the first class of students.

Oct. 29, 1929: Stock market crashes, plunging America into the Great Depression.

Perhaps best known for his lifelong commitment to feeding hungry people throughout the world

In 1931, things were getting a little better in the United States, but many banks in Europe failed. The problems in Europe hurt the U.S. economy. Hoover believed that the federal government had no choice but to step in and try to help. He created the Reconstruction Finance Corporation (RFC) to make loans to farmers, banks, businesses, and railroads.

The RFC helped many people. In doing this, it made rules that businesses had to follow. Hoover had always been against the government overseeing business in this way. But in such desperate times, he believed it was the only way to help the nation recover.

Although the RFC had some success, the Great Depression kept getting worse. By 1932, 12 million people were out of work. Many had lost their homes, too. They were forced to live in shacks made of scrap lumber or cardboard. These rundown "towns" were called "Hoovervilles."

Americans placed the blame for the Great Depression squarely on the shoulders of the president.

▼ *Many Americans without jobs lived in "Hoovervilles."*

In Hoover's four years as president, he went from being one of the most popular men in America to being one of the most hated presidents of all time.

The 1932 presidential election was approaching. When the Republicans chose Hoover to run again, he refused to spend time campaigning. He said that his time would be better spent trying to solve the nation's many problems.

The Democrat running against Hoover was Franklin D. Roosevelt, the governor of New York. Roosevelt was a charming man with a big, bright smile and a smooth, comforting voice. Americans were upset with Hoover and with how long it was taking for the economy to recover. They overwhelmingly elected Roosevelt president in 1932. He won forty-two of the forty-eight states. The Great Humanitarian was defeated by the Great Depression.

Herbert Hoover ▼ and political opponent Franklin D. Roosevelt

After the White House

★ ★ ★

Inspired to continue his life's work of feeding the hungry and helping young people, Hoover ran into difficulties in the months following his term as president. Hoover was blamed for causing the Great Depression, or at least doing nothing to solve America's great economic problems.

In 1934, however, he published a book called *The Challenge to Liberty,* which criticized the policies of President Roosevelt's New Deal. The book sold well and was considered Hoover's successful return to being an important part of American political dialogue.

Never one to sit still for long, Hoover itched to get back into public service. Joining the board of the Boys Clubs of America in 1936, he was soon chosen to be its chairman. Determined to help inner-city boys stay on the right path, he opened more than one hundred new Boys Clubs in the next three years, setting a goal of "A Thousand

Hoover in 1956 ▲ with members of the Boys Club during the group's fiftieth anniversary

Clubs for a Million Boys" for the organization.

Excluded from public policy decisions during the years of World War II (1939–1945) by Roosevelt, Hoover was welcomed back to the White House in 1945 by President Harry Truman. By 1946, Hoover had planted the seeds of a worldwide organization dedicated to feeding hungry children. This organization eventually grew into UNICEF (United Nations International Children's Emergency Fund).

A lifelong opponent of big government, Hoover helped
to simplify government agencies and the military for
Presidents Truman, Eisenhower, and Kennedy. Working
eight-to twelve-hour days even at the age of eighty-six, his
tireless efforts have had a lasting effect on the United States.

The man who was respected far more for his work out
of office than for his years as president died on October 20,
1964. He was ninety years old. (His wife, Lou, had died of
a heart attack twenty years earlier.) He had given fifty years

◀ *President Harry
Truman (left)
encouraged Hoover
to become involved
in government
again.*

of his life to public service. During that time he accepted no payment for his work. In a letter to a child, Hoover once wrote: "Being a politician is a poor profession. Being a public servant is a noble one."

Herbert Hoover, politician and public servant

GLOSSARY

★ ★ ★

allies—countries that support one another in a conflict

ambassador—the representative of a nation's government in another country

blockade—to keep a nation's ships from leaving or entering ports

diplomats—people who represent their government in a foreign country

distribute—to give things out; to deliver

engineering—using science and math to design products or control nature

geology—the science that deals with rocks and Earth's history

humanitarian—a person who works to help people and relieve suffering

inaugural address—a president's first speech after taking office

moral—relating to what is right and decent behavior

neutral—not supporting either side in an argument or a war

Quakers—people who belong to a Christian group called the Religious Society of Friends. Quakers reject war and stress peace education.

rebellion—an armed uprising against the government

sacrifice—to give up something important

standardize—to make something that meets accepted guidelines

HERBERT HOOVER'S LIFE AT A GLANCE

★ ★ ★

PERSONAL

Nickname:	Great Engineer, Great Humanitarian
Born:	August 10, 1874
Birthplace:	West Branch, Iowa
Father's name:	Jesse Clark Hoover
Mother's name:	Hulda Randall Minthorn Hoover
Education:	Graduated from Stanford University in 1895
Wife's name:	Lou Henry Hoover
Married:	February 10, 1899
Children:	Herbert Clark Hoover Jr. (1903–1969); Allan Henry Hoover (1907–1993)
Died:	October 20, 1964, in New York City, New York
Buried:	West Branch, Iowa

PUBLIC

Occupation before presidency:	Engineer
Occupation after presidency:	Statesman
Military service:	None
Other government positions:	Head of U.S. Food Administration (1917–1918); secretary of commerce
Political party:	Republican
Vice president:	Charles Curtis
Dates in office:	March 4, 1929–March 3, 1933
Presidential opponents:	Alfred E. Smith (Democrat), 1928; Franklin Delano Roosevelt (Democrat), 1932
Number of votes (Electoral College):	21,411,991 of 36,412,176 (444 of 531), 1928; 15,758,901 of 38,568,539 (51 of 531), 1932
Writings:	*The Challenge to Liberty* (1934), *America's First Crusade* (1943), *Memoirs* (3 vols., 1951–1952), *The Ordeal of Wilson* (1958), *An American Epic* (4 vols., 1959-1964), *On Growing Up* (1962), *Fishing for Fun* (1963)

★

Herbert Hoover's Cabinet

Secretary of state:
Henry L. Stimson (1929–1933)

Secretary of the treasury:
Andrew W. Mellon (1929–1932)
Ogden L. Mills (1932–1933)

Secretary of war:
James W. Good (1929)
Patrick J. Hurley (1929–1933)

Attorney general:
William DeWitt Mitchell
(1929–1933)

Postmaster general:
Walter F. Brown (1929–1933)

Secretary of the navy:
Charles F. Adams (1929–1933)

Secretary of the interior:
Ray L. Wilbur (1929–1933)

Secretary of agriculture:
Arthur M. Hyde (1929–1933)

Secretary of commerce:
Robert P. Lamont (1929–1932)
Roy D. Chapin (1932–1933)

Secretary of labor:
James J. Davis (1929–1930)
William N. Doak (1930–1933)

HERBERT HOOVER'S LIFE AND TIMES

★ ★ ★

HOOVER'S LIFE

August 10, Hoover (below, right) is born in West Branch, Iowa   **1874**

WORLD EVENTS

1876   The Battle of the Little Bighorn is a victory for Native Americans defending their homes in the West against General George Custer (above)

Alexander Graham Bell uses the first telephone to speak to his assistant, Thomas Watson

1877   German inventor Nikolaus A. Otto works on what will become the internal combustion engine for automobiles

HOOVER'S LIFE

Father, Jesse
Hoover, dies — 1880

Mother, Hulda
Hoover, dies — 1883

Moves to Newberg,
Oregon, (below) to live
with an uncle — 1884

Graduates from — 1895
Stanford University
in Palo Alto,
California

Begins working for a — 1897
mining company
in Australia

1880

1890

WORLD EVENTS

1882 — Thomas Edison builds
a power station

1884 — Mark Twain publishes
*The Adventures of
Huckleberry Finn*

1886 — Grover Cleveland
dedicates the Statue of
Liberty in New York

Bombing in
Haymarket
Square,
Chicago, due
to labor unrest
(right)

1893 — Women gain voting
privileges in New
Zealand, the first
country to take such a
step

1896 — The Olympic Games
are held for the first
time in recent history,
in Athens, Greece

HOOVER'S LIFE

Marries Lou Henry (left); begins working in China — 1899

Establishes his own engineering firm — 1908

Sets up the Commission for Relief in Belgium during World War I (below) — 1914–1917

Heads the U.S. Food Administration — 1917

WORLD EVENTS

1903 — Brothers Orville and Wilbur Wright successfully fly a powered airplane

1909 — The National Association for the Advancement of Colored People (NAACP) is founded

1913 — Henry Ford begins to use standard assembly lines to produce automobiles

1914 — Archduke Francis Ferdinand is assassinated, launching World War I (1914–1918)

1916 — German-born physicist Albert Einstein publishes his general theory of relativity

1917 — Vladimir Ilyich Lenin and Leon Trotsky lead Bolsheviks in a rebellion against the czars in Russia during the October Revolution

1900

1910

HOOVER'S LIFE

1920

President Warren G. Harding (left) names Hoover secretary of commerce — 1921

Presidential Election Results:	Popular Votes	Electoral Votes
1928 Herbert C. Hoover	21,411,991	444
Alfred E. Smith	15,000,185	87
1932 Franklin D. Roosevelt	22,809,638	472
Herbert C. Hoover	15,258,901	59

March 4, gives the first inaugural address broadcast nationally over the radio — 1929

October 29, the stock market crashes, starting the Great Depression

Congress passes the Hawley-Smoot Tariff—the highest tax on imports in U.S. history — 1930

1930

Creates the Reconstruction Finance Corporation (RFC) to provide government help to businesses — 1931

WORLD EVENTS

1920 — American women get the right to vote

1926 — A.A. Milne (right) publishes *Winnie the Pooh*

Claude Monet and Mary Cassat, well-known impressionist painters, die

1928 — Penicillin, the first antibiotic, is discovered by Scottish scientist Alexander Fleming

1930 — Designs for the first jet engine are submitted to the Patent Office in Britain

HOOVER'S LIFE

1932 15,000 World War I veterans march on Washington, D.C., demanding their bonus pay. After they riot, Hoover orders the U.S. Army to force them to leave.

Loses election to Franklin Delano Roosevelt

1934 Publishes *The Challenge to Liberty*

1936 Joins the Boys Clubs of America and opens more than one hundred clubs in the next three years

WORLD EVENTS

1933 Nazi leader Adolf Hitler (above) is named chancellor of Germany

1939 German troops invade Poland. Britain and France declare war on Germany. World War II (1939–45) begins

Commercial television is introduced to America

1941 December 7, Japanese bombers attack Pearl Harbor, Hawaii, (below) and America enters World War II

1940

HOOVER'S LIFE

Appointed by 1946
President Harry
Truman (left) as
coordinator of the
Food Supply for
World Famine, which
helps starving people
at the end of
World War II

Publishes his memoirs 1951–
1952

1950

1960

The Hoover 1962
Presidential Library is
dedicated in West
Branch, Iowa

October 20, 1964
Hoover dies

WORLD EVENTS

1942 Japanese Americans
are placed in intern-
ment camps due to
fear of disloyalty

1945 America drops atomic
bombs on the Japanese
cities of Hiroshima
and Nagasaki to end
World War II

The United Nations
is founded

1949 Birth of the People's
Republic of China

1953 The first
Europeans
climb Mount
Everest (right)

1963 Kenya becomes an
independent republic

1964 G.I. Joe makes his
debut as the first boy's
"action figure"

UNDERSTANDING HERBERT HOOVER AND HIS PRESIDENCY

★ ★ ★

IN THE LIBRARY

Holford, David M. *Herbert Hoover*. Springfield, N.J.: Enslow, 1999.

Joseph, Paul. *Herbert Hoover*. Minneapolis: Abdo & Daughters, 2001

Souter, Gerry, and Janet Souter. *Herbert Hoover, Our Thirty-First President*. Chanhassen, Minn.: The Child's World, 2001.

ON THE WEB

President Hoover on the Bonus Army
http://www.msys.net/cress/ballots2/bonus.htm
To read excerpts from Hoover's memoirs

The Herbert Hoover Presidential Library and Museum
http://hoover.archives.gov/kids/
For information on Hoover and games for kids

Internet Public Library—Herbert Hoover
http://www.ipl.org/ref/POTUS/hchoover.html
For information about Hoover's presidency and
many links to other resources

The American Presidency—Herbert Hoover

http://www.americanpresident.org/kotrain/courses/HH/HH_In_Brief.htm

For information and many links about Hoover and his presidency

The White House—Herbert Hoover

http://www.whitehouse.gov/history/presidents/hh31.html

For official information about Herbert Hoover on the
White House web site

Herbert Hoover National Historic Site

http://www.nps.gov/heho/

For a virtual tour of Hoover's birthplace

HOOVER HISTORIC SITES
ACROSS THE COUNTRY

**Herbert Hoover
National Historic Site**
110 Parkside Drive
P.O. Box 607
West Branch, IA 52358-0607
319/643-2541
To visit Hoover's birthplace

**Herbert Hoover Presidential
Library and Museum**
210 Parkside Drive
P.O. Box 488
West Branch, IA 52538
319/643-5301
To visit the library and museum
devoted to the lives of Herbert
Hoover and his wife, Lou Henry
Hoover, and their many years of
public service

Hoover-Minthorn House
Hazel and Highland
Salem, OR 97132
503/538-6629
To visit the home where young
Herbert Hoover lived with his
aunt and uncle after the death
of his parents

THE U.S. PRESIDENTS
(Years in Office)

★ ★ ★

1. George Washington
   (March 4, 1789-March 3, 1797)
2. John Adams
   (March 4, 1797-March 3, 1801)
3. Thomas Jefferson
   (March 4, 1801-March 3, 1809)
4. James Madison
   (March 4, 1809-March 3, 1817)
5. James Monroe
   (March 4, 1817-March 3, 1825)
6. John Quincy Adams
   (March 4, 1825-March 3, 1829)
7. Andrew Jackson
   (March 4, 1829-March 3, 1837)
8. Martin Van Buren
   (March 4, 1837-March 3, 1841)
9. William Henry Harrison
   (March 6, 1841-April 4, 1841)
10. John Tyler
    (April 6, 1841-March 3, 1845)
11. James K. Polk
    (March 4, 1845-March 3, 1849)
12. Zachary Taylor
    (March 5, 1849-July 9, 1850)
13. Millard Fillmore
    (July 10, 1850-March 3, 1853)
14. Franklin Pierce
    (March 4, 1853-March 3, 1857)
15. James Buchanan
    (March 4, 1857-March 3, 1861)
16. Abraham Lincoln
    (March 4, 1861-April 15, 1865)
17. Andrew Johnson
    (April 15, 1865-March 3, 1869)

18. Ulysses S. Grant
    (March 4, 1869-March 3, 1877)
19. Rutherford B. Hayes
    (March 4, 1877-March 3, 1881)
20. James Garfield
    (March 4, 1881-Sept 19, 1881)
21. Chester Arthur
    (Sept 20, 1881-March 3, 1885)
22. Grover Cleveland
    (March 4, 1885-March 3, 1889)
23. Benjamin Harrison
    (March 4, 1889-March 3, 1893)
24. Grover Cleveland
    (March 4, 1893-March 3, 1897)
25. William McKinley
    (March 4, 1897-
    September 14, 1901)
26. Theodore Roosevelt
    (September 14, 1901-
    March 3, 1909)
27. William Howard Taft
    (March 4, 1909-March 3, 1913)
28. Woodrow Wilson
    (March 4, 1913-March 3, 1921)
29. Warren G. Harding
    (March 4, 1921-August 2, 1923)
30. Calvin Coolidge
    (August 3, 1923-March 3, 1929)
31. Herbert Hoover
    (March 4, 1929-March 3, 1933)
32. Franklin D. Roosevelt
    (March 4, 1933-April 12, 1945)

33. Harry S. Truman
    (April 12, 1945-
    January 20, 1953)
34. Dwight D. Eisenhower
    (January 20, 1953-
    January 20, 1961)
35. John F. Kennedy
    (January 20, 1961-
    November 22, 1963)
36. Lyndon B. Johnson
    (November 22, 1963-
    January 20, 1969)
37. Richard M. Nixon
    (January 20, 1969-
    August 9, 1974)
38. Gerald R. Ford
    (August 9, 1974-
    January 20, 1977)
39. James Earl Carter
    (January 20, 1977-
    January 20, 1981)
40. Ronald Reagan
    (January 20, 1981-
    January 20, 1989)
41. George H. W. Bush
    (January 20, 1989-
    January 20, 1993)
42. William Jefferson Clinton
    (January 20, 1993-
    January 20, 2001)
43. George W. Bush
    (January 20, 2001-)

INDEX

★ ★ ★

ABOUT THE AUTHOR

Michael Teitelbaum has been writing and editing children's books and magazines for more than twenty years. He was editor of *Little League Magazine for Kids* and is the author of a two-volume encyclopedia on the Baseball Hall of Fame. Michael has also written many books based on popular cartoon characters such as Garfield and Batman. He recently adapted the films *Spider-Man* and *Men In Black II* into junior novels. Michael and his wife, Sheleigah, split their time between New York City and their 160-year-old farmhouse in the Catskill Mountains of upstate New York.

9|05	2	11|03
6-16	3	3-15
1|20	3	——
2|23	3	3|15
8|24	3	3|15

BAKER & TAYLOR